The Hermeneutical Flaws of Dispensationalism

Gary George

The Hermeneutical Flaws of Dispensationalism

Gary George

NEWCOVENANT
MEDIA

5317 Wye Creek Drive, Frederick, MD 21703-6938
301-473-8781 | info@newcovenantmedia.com
www.NewCovenantMedia.com

The Hermeneutical Flaws of Dispensationalism

Table of Contents

Introduction

By John G. Reisinger

Every system of theology has its own principles of interpretation. Each system shares some hermeneutical presuppositions with other systems; each has areas of difference. Historically, two schools of systematic theology have articulated the major areas of difference among evangelical Christians. Covenant Theology and Dispensational Theology agree on basic tenets such as the existence and nature of God and the inspiration of Scripture, but disagree on methods of interpreting the Scripture, especially the prophetic passages. New Covenant Theology, a third, distinct systematic option, shares the fundamental doctrines of God and Scripture with both Covenant Theology and Dispensational Theology, but differs from both in its hermeneutics. New Covenant Theology grounds its interpretive principles on the way in which Christ and the writers of the New Testament understood and used the Old Testament.

Other works in recent years have begun to compare the differences between New Covenant Theology and Covenant Theology.[1] *The Hermeneutical Flaws of Dispensationalism*

---

[1] Richard Barcellos, *In Defense of The Decalogue: A Critique Of New Covenant Theology* (Enumclaw, WA: WinePress Publishing, 2001). Tom

examines one area where New Covenant Theology differs from Dispensationalism. Using a redemptive-historical approach derived from the New Testament writers' interpretation of the Old Testament, New Covenant Theology challenges Dispensationalism's literal (natural) hermeneutic for understanding Old Testament kingdom prophecy. The author of this work, Gary George, lists five promises made in the Old Testament Scriptures that New Covenant Theology, with Covenant Theology, believes are spiritually fulfilled now, in the church.

another temple (Zech. 6:12, 13)

another priest (Ps. 110:4)

another king (2 Sam. 7:12-14)

another prophet (Deut. 18:15)

another covenant (Jer. 31:31-34)

George provides ample New Testament evidence to support a current true spiritual fulfillment for each of the five points. However, an important question remains: Does a clear, present spiritual fulfillment of a specific Old Testament prophecy in the New Testament Scriptures automatically rule out the possibility of a natural fulfillment of that same prophecy in the future? Do the Scriptures sometimes indicate both a natural and a spiritual fulfillment of the same prophecy? In our answer, we must be careful not

---

Wells and Fred Zaspel, *New Covenant Theology: Description, Definition, Defense* (Frederick, MD: New Covenant Media, 2002). John G. Reisinger, *In Defense of Jesus, the New Lawgiver* (Frederick, MD: New Covenant Media, 2008).

to go past what Scripture actually says; likewise, we dare not resent anyone who would answer this question differently than we would answer it.

Unless we put God in a box of our own making, we must admit that *it is possible* that all five of the above prophecies could have a double fulfillment: a spiritual one now and a natural one in a post-church age. Probably everyone would agree that the church is the true temple, the dwelling place of God (1 Cor. 3), built in fulfillment of the promise made in Zechariah 6 and 2 Samuel 7:13. Does this fulfillment preclude the possible construction of the literal temple of stone described in Ezekiel 40-42? Fulfillment in one realm may not inherently eliminate the possibility of fulfillment in another realm.

George believes that the present spiritual fulfillment of the five *anothers* is more than sufficient to fulfill the Old Testament prophecies, and he sees no necessity of a future physical temple, priest, king, prophet, or covenant. Just because we believe the prophecy has been clearly fulfilled once spiritually, thereby eliminating the need for a future physical temple does not necessarily mean that God cannot have a physical one built in the future. We hasten to add, though, that if a person is going to hold double-fulfillment of the temple promise, or any of the other *anothers*, as an article of faith, he needs positive evidence from the New Testament Scriptures. Believing that something is a possibility and believing that something is a specific promise in Scripture are two different things.

We should not speak about a future, second, natural fulfillment of any of the above five promises if we have openly acknowledged that all five have already been spiritually fulfilled. People who acknowledge that all of these things have been spiritually fulfilled and who also advocate another fulfillment bear the onus to do one of two things. (1) They must furnish New Testament evidence for any valid hope of a natural fulfillment in the future, or (2) they must admit that their entire system of understanding prophecy is based on forcing the New Testament Scriptures to fit a natural interpretation of the Old Testament Scriptures, instead of allowing the New Testament Scriptures to interpret Old Testament prophecy. New Covenant Theology does not find New Testament evidence for a double fulfillment of the Old Testament promises of another temple, priest, king, prophet or covenant; therefore, we do not hold double fulfillment as an article of faith. This is a key area where we differ from Dispensationalism.

One need only compare the Old Scofield Reference Bible (1909 and 1917) with the New Scofield Reference edition (1967) to discover alterations to a number of Dispensational footnotes. Some of these alterations change the character of Dispensationalism to the extent that the term Dispensationalist may no longer be legitimate for some adherents to use. A new brand of Dispensationalism calls itself *Progressive Dispensationalism* and openly denies what seems to many to be the very building blocks of the system. Gary George's purpose in this work is not to chart the migration of Dispensationalism from its early roots to its present position, but to examine biblically the basic hermeneutical presupposition of any and all systems of Dispensationalism. Whether we discuss Darby, Scofield, Ryrie, or Dallas Theological Seminary, we find some basic tenets common to any system of Dispensationalism.

Gary George and I, along with many other believers, boasted for years that we were free from creeds and denominations and were students of Scripture alone. Little did we realize that just as the various denominations had done, we too had accepted, lock, stock, and barrel, a man-made system of theology. Even as we declared that we were free from any influence other than the teachings of the Holy Spirit, we were unconsciously wedded to a system of thought. The stark reality is that multitudes of saints unwittingly read the Scriptures through a ready-made, hand-me-down theology set before them by revered men. Other believers acknowledge human teachers (1 Cor. 1:12; 3:4) and faithfully follow their interpretations, deeming those teachers to be such gifts to the church that to ignore them would be akin to blaspheming the Holy Spirit. If ever anyone deserved such a following, the apostle Paul would have been the man. Knowing the propensities of humans to seek security in the wisdom of men, he beseeched his new converts to continue in the grace of God (Acts 13:43), that they might learn not to think of men above that which is written (1 Cor. 4:6).

It has been noted that in the last few centuries, three Johns have had a great influence on the Christian church: John Calvin, John Wesley, and John Darby. For the majority of Christians, the first two are familiar names; the last, whose contributions to Christian doctrine may have had the widest penetration, remains largely unknown. Darby, generally accepted as the father of Dispensationalism, had a profound impact on the author of this work. Few realize that the better-known teachers of the system are indebted to J. N. Darby for his articulations of Dispensational doctrines. In the 1830s, Darby introduced teachings largely unknown to historic Christianity. Darby's teachings (as well as those of other Plymouth Brethren teachers) have been somewhat modified and diversified in differing degrees among Dispensationalists today.[2] Most no longer have a system of interpretation as rigid as the one originally posited, nor do they hold a dogmatic monolith. The focus of this work is on the strictest of this group, namely, Darby's Dispensationalism. Therefore, not all Dispensationalists who read the following will identify with the criticisms made on a number of points.

Gary George's work addresses the crucial issue of principles of interpretation. How do we understand what the Old Testament prophecies mean? Do we read a specific prophecy, figure out its natural meaning, and then measure every pertinent New Testament passage by that Old Tes-

---

[2] Craig Blaising defines three periods of Dispensationalism's history of transition: the classical period of 1878 - 1940s; the revised period of the 1950s - 1970s; and the progressive period of the 1980s – present. Herbert W. Bateman IV, ed., *Three Central Issues in Contemporary Dispensationalism* (Grand Rapids, MI: Kregel Publications, 1999), 23.

tament natural understanding to see if that prophecy has been fulfilled? When Peter, in Acts 2, said, "This is that," did he mean that (1) the prophecy of Joel *has been fulfilled,* or (2) because the actual events of Pentecost do not seem to meet the natural fulfillment criteria of our Old Testament interpretation, the events that occurred on Pentecost are only a *type of a future literal fulfillment?* John MacArthur provides an example of Dispensational interpretation: the second understanding of Peter's statement.

Acts 2:16-21: See introduction to Joel: Interpretive Challenges; see notes on Joel 2:28-32. Joel's prophecy will not be completely fulfilled until the millennial kingdom and the final judgment. But Peter, by using it, shows that Pentecost was a pre-fulfillment, a taste of what will happen in the millennial kingdom when the Spirit is poured on all flesh (cf. 10:45).[3]

Is that what Peter meant by "this is that which was spoken by the prophet Joel"?

One of Paul's statements about his imprisonment illustrates the way in which New Covenant Theology addresses how to interpret Old Testament kingdom prophecy. Paul said that he was "bound in chains" because of his preaching the hope of Israel (Acts 28:20). A careful analysis of Paul's preaching for its content reveals exactly what Paul considered the true hope of the Israelite. If we look closely at what Paul, and every other New Testament writer, has

[3] *The MacArthur Study Bible,* ed., John MacArthur, (Nashville: Word Bible, 1997), 1635. See also pages 1268 and 1272.

to say about the temple, the priest, the king, the prophet, and the covenant, we find that they always speak of these things as present realities that have fulfilled the Old Testament prophecies. We do not have a single instance in the New Testament Scriptures where a writer gives the slightest hope to a Jew to expect still *another* temple, *another* priest, *another* king, *another* prophet, or *another* covenant. The uniform message in the New Testament Scriptures is that Israel's hope has been fulfilled in the promised Messiah.

Peter explains the miraculous healing of the lame man at the Beautiful Gate in terms of prophetic fulfillment:

"Indeed, all the prophets from Samuel on, as many as have spoken, have foretold these days. And you are heirs of the prophets and of the covenant God made with your fathers. He said to Abraham, 'Through your offspring all peoples on earth will be blessed.' When God raised up his servant, he sent him first to you to bless you by turning each of you from your wicked ways." (Acts 3:24-26, NIV)

It is *these days*, not a future earthly millennium, of which the Old Testament prophets spoke. Every believer under the New Covenant is the true heir of the prophets and the covenant made with Abraham. The Father sent the resurrected Lord to bless the true people of God with the true Abrahamic blessing, namely, forgiveness of sins. We will search the New Testament Scriptures in vain for a promise of *another* temple, *another* priest, *another* king, *another* prophet, or *another* covenant that in any way involves the physical land of Palestine or the physical nation of Israel.

In Acts 13, after giving a short history of God's dealing with Israel, Paul applied this truth to his audience.

"We tell you the good news: What God promised our fathers he has fulfilled for us, their children, by raising up Jesus. As it is written in the second Psalm: 'You are my Son; today I have become your Father.' The fact that God raised him from the dead, never to decay, is stated in these words: 'I will give you the holy and sure blessings promised to David.'" (Acts 13:32-34, NIV)

What "God promised the [Jewish] fathers" does not wait for a future fulfillment. The true people of God, the church, have inherited the "sure blessings promised to David." I repeat my earlier statement: spiritual fulfillment of the promised blessings now does not automatically rule out a natural fulfillment in the future. The church's present possession of the sure mercies of David does not prove without question that the prophecy cannot have a double fulfillment: one spiritual and one natural. However, with Gary George, I insist on clear New Testament evidence before such a hope can have a valid foundation.

If nothing else comes from reading this work other than a desire for a more scrutinizing search of the Scriptures, we will have accomplished at least one of our main goals. "It is good to be zealously affected" (Gal. 4:18), "even if through my lie, God's truth abounds" (Rom. 3:7, ESV).

Author's Preface

I had been an avid supporter of J. N. Darby's (1800-1882) Classic Dispensationalism for eleven of my sixteen years among the Plymouth Brethren; I abandoned it almost twenty-five years ago. As a dissident of Classic Dispensationalism, I am not surprised to hear that prominent men have renounced that weak theological system. My own switch originated in August 1986, not by means of men's writings, but through a commentary-less study in the Book of Romans. My study on that occasion was without the aid of Brethren authors; however, their influence keenly, albeit unconsciously, guided my interpretation. As I approached the last chapter of Romans, one sentence halted my study, gave me a profound shock, and eventually put me in great disharmony with my beloved Plymouth Brethren.

"Now to him that is of power to establish you according to my gospel, and the preaching of Jesus Christ, according to the revelation of the mystery, which was kept secret since the world began, but now is made manifest, and by the scriptures of the prophets, according to the commandment of the everlasting God, made known to all nations for the obedience of faith: To God, only wise, be glory through Jesus Christ forever. Amen." (Romans 16:25-27)

To my amazement, this passage seemed to say something different from what I had always understood it to mean. I had believed, as my Dispensational mentors had taught, that "the mystery...now is made manifest, and by the **scriptures** of the prophets..." meant the **New Testament Scriptures**. I now saw those words in a different light. For the first time, I realized that Paul was talking about the Old Testament Scriptures, not the New Testament Scriptures. From a Classic Dispensational viewpoint, such a conclusion is untenable. Recognizing the consequences of such a conviction, I determined to go through Romans again. This time I would pay closer attention to the more than sixty Old Testament quotations to see if the prophets of old had indeed predicted what occurred in the apostles' day, or whether this present age was an unforeseen parenthesis.

Turning back to the first chapter of Romans, I realized that the first two verses confirmed my could-be-new-heresy. "...the gospel of God (which he had promised afore [O.T.] by his prophets in the Holy Scriptures)..." (Rom. 1:1-2). I was almost afraid to read further for fear that what I might find would destroy my career and relationships among the Brethren and other fellow Dispensationalists. Nevertheless, I continued to read, seeking to believe all things written in the Book, even if the consequences of what I believed distanced me from the most esteemed of saints. For me, the Roman epistle settled the verdict; I saw not only there, but also everywhere throughout the New Testament Scriptures, that the church and church age is indeed the subject of prophecy in the Old Testament Scriptures.

The thought of eventually having to inform my brethren of my abandonment of Dispensationalism was not pleasant: I knew my change could alienate us. Such a change would be similar to a Catholic priest's confession to his parishioners that he believed in Protestantism. I knew, however, that I could not continue in a system that contained such a fundamental error.

All error is serious, but not all error is equally serious. The error promoted by the historic Dispensationalist is of a very serious nature indeed. This branch of Dispensationalism so radically divides the two testaments that it supposes not only two different peoples of God, but also two different kinds of callings, and two different destinies for Old and New Testament believers. The practical dimension of this theology results in making parts of the New Testament irrelevant to the church reader. Consider Clarence Larkin's note on this subject: "The new covenant has not yet been made. It is to be made with Israel after they get back to their own land. It is promised in Jeremiah 31:31-37. It is unconditional and will cover the millennium and the new heaven and new earth. It is based on the finished work of Christ, Matthew 26:28. **It has nothing to do with the church and does not belong to this Dispensation.**"[4]

Another significant way in which this system of interpretation injures the truth is the manner in which it con-

---

[4] Clarence Larkin, *Dispensational Truth* (Philadelphia, PA: Rev. Clarence Larkin est., 1918): 151, quoted in Bateman, *Three Central Issues*, 31, emphasis added.

strues the offices of Christ. John Gerstner put it well: "Dar-by, with his penchant for historical division and separation, viewed these offices as successive rather than simultane-ous. Christ was a prophet while on earth, a priest in heav-en, and a king in the kingdom yet to come."[5] If a system of theology denies any of what Scripture attributes to Christ, it strips him of those glories that are rightfully his and lim-its the church's vocabulary for expressions of admiration in their worship of Christ.

Approximately one-tenth of the New Testament directly or indirectly quotes or alludes to the Old Testament. The New Testament authors' frequent use of the Old Testament raises important questions about the relationship of the two testaments:

How does biblical revelation develop?

What is the meaning of fulfillment?

Darby/Scofieldism deflects the intent of what the proph-ets predicted concerning the blessing of the entire world during the church age.

This system of interpretation presents a dilemma: while it ignores parts of Scripture, it seems to provide (superfi-cially) a solution to problems raised by other parts of Scrip-ture, such as imprecatory Psalms and Old Testament ethi-cal standards far below New Testaments norms. On the one hand, the system is erroneous; but on the other hand,

---

[5] John Gerstner, *Wrongly Dividing the Word of Truth* (Brentwood, TN: Wolgemuth & Hyatt, 1991), 117.

parts of it are helpful. Historically, the entrance of Darby/Scofield Dispensationalism stirred the stagnant waters of Covenant Theology and generated serious Bible discussion among thoughtful interpreters. This discussion promoted a renewed examination of the issue of continuity and discontinuity, and contributed to the current debate among biblical scholars from both schools. New Covenant Theology takes a fresh look at the discussion and offers a third voice, previously unheard in the debate. All three schools of theology must constantly examine their presuppositions to comply with the biblical mandate to prove all things.

The debate will likely continue until the Lord returns; we hope that until then, all parties will strive for a biblically scholastic median that humbly recognizes that "we know in part and we prophesy in part...for we see now through a dim window obscurely, but then, face to face" (1 Cor. 13:9, 12, J. N. Darby's translation). Even though some Brethren I dearly loved labeled me as a semi-heretic, I have produced the following pages, not vindictively, but lovingly. Some of the godliest brothers and sisters I have known were in the Brethren movement. "Let nothing be done through strife or vainglory, but in lowliness of mind let each esteem others better than themselves" (Phil. 2:3).

Prophetic Fulfillment

The authors of the New Testament mention two major covenants: an Old Covenant and a New Covenant that replaces the old one (Heb. 8:1-13 and Gal. 4:24). The first covenant was with Israel after the flesh, mediated through Moses at Mount Sinai (1 Cor. 10:18 and Heb. 9:18-20). Some theologians believe the second covenant was with the same Israel, but others insist it was with the church, through Christ. That the first covenant was abrogated is beyond dispute (Heb. 8:13), but whether the second is actuated in the New Testament church or remains to be realized with the nation of Israel in the future is the concern of the following pages. For many, such an issue may seem insignificant; for an intellectual Dispensationalist, the matter is crucial.

Classic Dispensationalists believe that we must regard the installation of the second covenant as in abeyance or suspension until its formal and expected establishment with national Israel in the future. Although the church presently enjoys moral blessings and spiritual benefits based solely upon the blood of the New Covenant, she is not the intended heir. "...Although certain features of this covenant have been fulfilled for believers in the present Church Age...the covenant *remains to be realized* for Israel according to the explicit statement of v. 31."[6] Dispensation-alists are constrained to make this confession because of hermeneutical assumptions drawn from a collation of certain Bible texts that stake out the boundaries for Dispensational Theology. The foremost of these assumptions is that in order to be fulfilled, Old Testament prophecy must have its literal (natural) parallel in the New Testament Scriptures. The New Testament church age does not meet (or seem to meet) this standard of interpretation; therefore, the prophecies must be construed as postponed to a future time.[7] Dispensationalism's understanding of Paul's statement of the "...mystery...hid in God" and "...hid from ages..." (Eph. 3:9 and Col. 1:26) develops from this tenet. Because the mystery was unknown, the Old Testament writers could not prophesy about it; therefore, the corpus of Old Testament literature does not predict the church (and the church age). The church age is a parenthesis.

Another facet of this doctrinal view is the belief in a two-stage coming of Christ that allows an interval of time after the church is raptured (the first stage) for a revival of ancient Israel. This two-stage return permits the nation of Israel to receive the second covenant along with other Jew-

---

[6] Footnote on Jeremiah 31:31, in *The New Scofield Reference Bible*, ed., C. I. Scofield, (NY: Oxford University Press, 1967), 804, emphasis added.

[7] Some kind of a postponement of the fulfillment of specific Old Covenant blessings to the nation of Israel is essential to any and every form of Dispensationalism.

ish-designated promises before the final stage, when Christ comes in judgment. The *New Scofield* footnotes for the prophecy in Daniel 9:24-27 set the church age as an interim between the first and second advents of Christ. "The proof that this final week has not yet been fulfilled is seen in the fact that Christ definitely relates its main events to His second coming (Matt. 24:6, 15). Hence, during the interim between the sixty-ninth and seventieth weeks, there must lie the whole period of the Church set forth in the NT, but not revealed in the OT...."[8]

The particular issue at hand is whether Scripture demonstrates that the New Testament church is the New Covenant community of the last age, predicted in the Old Testament. If evidence exists to verify a positive answer to this question, then we must modify, if not nullify, the Dispensational concept of the Israel/church dichotomy to satisfy the biblical data. The relationship of Israel and the church is best expressed, not by a replacement theory, where the church takes the place of Israel, but by a theology of promise/fulfillment, where the church is the true goal toward which God has been working since Genesis 3:15. God has not postponed any of his sovereign purposes; he has not changed horses in the middle of the stream and replaced Israel with the church. Instead, he has created an entirely new entity, the body of Christ or "new man" (Eph. 2:13-16) made up of believing Jews and believing Gentiles. Paul calls it a "new creation" (2 Cor. 5:17). Although the

---

[8] *The New Scofield Reference Bible*, 913.

church, viewed as the body of Christ, was a new entry on the time-line of redemptive history, we must see that the Old Testament Scriptures as well as the New Testament Scriptures indicate that she has been God's unchanging purpose and goal from the beginning. The concept of the church as the New Covenant community was latent in the Old Testament Scriptures and is fully developed and unveiled in the New Testament Scriptures.

Sound exegesis harmonizes the Old Testament *with* the greater light of the New Testament; faulty exegesis isolates Old Testament passages *from* the New Testament. To be definite about the teaching of an Old Testament text, New Covenant Theology relies on the commentary of the New Testament as authoritative and final. The oft-quoted saying, "The new is in the old concealed, and the old is in the new revealed," reminds us of this interpretive method. I cannot overemphasize the significance of this approach to Scripture. This hermeneutic is the watershed point where Dispensational Theology and New Covenant Theology divide.

The Dispensationalist imposes a preconceived ecclesiological/eschatological system of interpretation on texts and thus often supersedes the primary sense that many New Testament writers give to an Old Testament passage. Dispensationalists and their opponents disagree over when to interpret a passage literally and when to interpret it figuratively. One's understanding of the meaning of Old Testament texts cited in the New Testament should be determined by the natural (face value) sense that the New Testament authors give to Old Testament citations. Dispensationalism is often compelled to strain the reasonable interpretation of certain New Testament texts in order to maintain a natural or literal meaning of the corresponding Old Testament texts. This methodology maintains the hermeneutical tenet that prohibits the spiritualization of any Old Testament kingdom prophecy. This occurs even when the New Testament writer has spiritualized the Old Testament kingdom passage. The Dispensational perspective ignores the plain meaning of a New Testament writer when that writer's interpretation of an Old Testament kingdom prophecy is contrary to Dispensational presuppositions. They must employ this method of interpretation in order to maintain a natural or double fulfillment approach to Old Testament prophecy.

We might ask, "Why is it legitimate for a New Testament writer to spiritualize an Old Testament prophecy, but not legitimate for us to accept the New Testament writer's spiritualized interpretation?" The kinds of prophecies to which I refer are not the predictive prophecies, such as Matthew 2 and Micah 5, but are the passages that deal primarily with the kingdom. Do New Testament writers sometimes naturalize kingdom prophecies, or do they uniformly spiritualize them? The following pages will develop and explain this concept of spiritual fulfillment.

The very body of literature that administers the Old Covenant indicates the transience of that era. The Old Testament Scriptures mention:

another temple (Zech. 6:12, 13)

another priest (Ps. 110:4)

another king (2 Sam. 7:12-14)

another prophet (Deut. 18:15)

another covenant (Jer. 31:31-34)

These five predictions verify that Old Testament authors clearly expected another and better era in the future. Does the New Testament church period meet and fulfill these expectations, or is that era still future? If the church (and church age) fulfills these prophecies, is there yet another literal (natural) fulfillment in the future? The Dispensationalist, using a passage like Romans 9:4, responds that the church has no definite claim to these five promises: the covenants, priests, temples, prophets, and kings belong to national Israel alone. How does the Dispensational view fare in the light of the entirety of New Testament teaching? We must depend on the inerrant authority of the New Testament Scriptures in order to draw the right conclusion.

Another Temple

"Behold the man whose name is the Branch...he shall build the temple ['house' in the LXX] of the LORD." (Zech. 6:12b)

"I will set up thy seed after thee.... He shall build an house for My name, and I will establish the throne of his kingdom...." (2 Sam. 7:12b, 13)

"...will I raise up the tabernacle of David..." (Amos 9:11)

Three questions about this temple need clear answers.

Do the New Testament Scriptures see these prophecies as already spiritually fulfilled? The answer is yes.

Do the New Testament Scriptures teach that there will not also be a natural fulfillment of the prophecies? The answer is no.

Do the New Testament Scriptures give any evidence or hope that there will be a second, natural fulfillment of these prophecies? The answer is no.

So where does that leave us? The three questions with their answers show that we have established one important tenet. There is no evidence in the New Testament Scriptures upon which Dispensationalists may ground their hope of a second fulfillment of another temple in a future age. Dispensationalists must draw their expectancy for a future temple from their own system of hermeneutics applied to the Old Testament Scriptures.

The builder mentioned in each of the above verses is Jesus the Messiah. Not everyone agrees, however, about **what** he is building and **when** he will build it. Dispensationalists state that the architecture to which all these verses refer is a physical structure in the forthcoming millennial age. If their statement is true, Jesus will return to carpentry and, with hammer and nails, actually construct a physical edifice, i.e., the temple prophesied in Zechariah 6:12b, 13 and described in Ezekiel 40-42.

The New Testament cites several instances of Jesus as a builder. Witnesses heard Jesus say, "I will build another [temple] made without hands" (Mark 14:58, cf. Acts 6:14). John records this saying in his gospel, "Jesus answered, and said unto them, 'Destroy this temple [Herod's], and in three days I will raise it up'" (John 2:19).

What will Jesus raise? Verse 21 answers the question: "He spoke of the temple of his body." Paul's language in Ephesians 1:22, 23 is reminiscent: "...the church, which is his body." Is the church the temple of Zechariah's prophecy to which John refers? Of all the New Testament authors, John alone uses Zechariah's word of exclamation – "behold" – in reference to the Lord Jesus:

> *"Behold, thy King cometh, sitting on an ass's colt."* (John 12:15; Zech. 9:9)

> *"They shall look on [behold] Him whom they pierced."* (John 19:37; Zech. 12:10)

> *"Behold the man."* (John 19:5; Zech. 6:12)

Another correlation between Zechariah and John is the mention of the word *branch*. Again, John alone among the gospel writers records Jesus' description of himself as the true vine that has many branches. These parallels are not coincidental, but intentional; they stem from divine design to provide the meaning of the branch's temple in Zechariah.

> In Him it is ordained to raise
> A temple to Jehovah's praise
> Composed of all the saints who own
> No Saviour but the "Living Stone."
> View the vast building, see it rise;
> The work how great! the plan how wise!
> O wondrous fabric! power unknown!
> That rears it on the "Living Stone."
>
> (P. Ritter 1760-1846)

Paul confirms that the church is this temple by combining several Old Testament prophetic passages and giving them present realization. "Ye are the temple of the living God; as God hath said, I will dwell in them, and walk in them; and I will be their God and they shall be my people" (2 Cor. 6:16b, cf. Ezek. 37:27; Jer. 31:33; Zech. 8:8). Paul's direct reference to the Corinthian believers as the temple of God (1 Cor. 3:16) is evidence that the promise in the Old Testament Scriptures of another temple has been fulfilled. If, in a future earthly millennium subsequent to this age, Jesus Christ rebuilds Zechariah's physical temple, double fulfillment will have occurred. Nevertheless, we need New Testament evidence in order to make that an article of faith. Because I do not see a necessity for a literal (natural) fulfillment in Scripture of the 'another temple' prophecy (the New Testament Scriptures show the prophecy is already fulfilled in a spiritual manner), that does not prove that a second and natural fulfillment may not occur. However, we are discussing not possibilities, but prophetic certainties. The key question is, do the New Covenant Scriptures ever, in any way, hold out the expectation of still another temple in addition to the church, or are passages such as the following the uniform message of the New Covenant Scriptures?

> *"Indeed, all the prophets from Samuel on, as many as have spoken, have foretold these days. And you are heirs of the prophets and of the covenant God made with your fathers. He said to Abraham, 'Through your offspring all peoples on earth will be blessed.' When God raised up his servant, he sent him first to you to bless you by turning each of you from your wicked ways."* (Acts 3:24-26, NIV)

The apostle Peter spoke these words to early church believers who were Jewish. His message is clear. (1) All of the Old Covenant prophets spoke of the days in which we now live and not of a different future day, and (2) the blessing promised Abraham is fulfilled in the person and work of the Messiah in this present age. Peter does not hint that they have some glorious future blessings in a post-church kingdom age. Any valid hope that a Jew has is in looking back to the fulfilled promises at the cross; it is not in looking forward to future earthly hopes.

Steven acknowledges the same thing when he cites Isaiah 66:1, "What house will ye build Me?" as he pointedly tells the Sanhedrin that God does not dwell in temples made with hands. Other New Testament writers repeat this idea (Acts 7:48, cf. Paul in Acts 17:24, Eph. 2:22, and John in Rev. 21:22). Isaiah, speaking from the divine point of view, has asked a rhetorical question, "The heaven is my throne, and the earth is my footstool. Where is the house that ye build unto me?" In the light of these passages, how can Dispensationalists believe that a millennial temple is in the minds of the authors of either the Old or New Testament Scriptures? The Scriptures themselves indicate the inadequacy of a three-dimensional place for God to dwell.

The entire book of Hebrews confirms that the present church is the single final dwelling place to which Old Testament prophecy referred. Hebrews 9:1 precludes the idea of a future clay and mortar temple: "The first covenant had also ordinances of divine service and a worldly sanctuary." The first covenant has vanished; so also has the possibility of another worldly sanctuary, bound up with that first covenant's ordinances of service (Col. 2:14; Eph. 2:15). Now that Christ and his writing disciples have introduced us to a better temple, "not pitched with man's hands," a return to a system of carnal ordinances signifying the not-yet-open way into the holiest place would reverse the economies of God. The better things would have to give way to the inferior things.

Because Christ has come as the antitype of all the former images and shadows of previous dispensations, we must concede that the good things formerly pictured are *now in existence* (Heb. 9:11, NEB, RSV, NIV). The Old Testament saints with their feeble economic administrations of the kingdom never received the promise; they could not be perfected without those saints who live in the New Testament-age of the kingdom (Heb. 11:40, cf. Mark 1:14, 15). The New Covenant church is the wondrous miracle of Christ's work; the New Covenant church is she "upon whom the end of the ages is come" (1 Cor. 10:11). For Dispensationalism then to expect a forthcoming concrete edifice, is, in essence, to rebuild the things that Christ destroyed and to make oneself a transgressor (Heb. 13:13).

The second verse cited under the heading for this section also points to the Messiah's work of building: "I will set up thy seed after thee.... He shall build an house for My name, and I will establish the throne of his kingdom...." (2 Sam. 7:12b, 13). We know that Solomon was not the intended fulfiller of this prophecy, in spite of the magnificent temple he erected. In Matthew, Jesus classifies himself as greater-than-Solomon and later states, "I will build my church and...the kingdom of heaven...." (Matt. 12:42 and 16:18, 19). Dispensationalists will not allow the church of which Jesus speaks to be the house that David's son would build. To do this, they would have to renounce the idea of a post-resurrection Jewish age when these prophecies are supposed to have their day.

We may safely follow the biblical authors' lead and equate the word *church* with the word *house*. Paul writes, "...the house of God, which is the church of the living God" (1 Tim. 3:15). In Hebrews, the author views the saints corporately as a house, "Christ as son over his own house, whose house are we...." (Heb. 3:6). Are Dispensationalists biblically justified in refusing to accept the church (or house) that Jesus said he would build as the fulfillment of Nathan's prophecy to David? In Matthew, the gospel of the king, Jesus is called the Son of David eight times, compared to only five times in all the other gospels combined. When we read Matthew's record of Jesus' statement, "I will build my church," we must understand his point in light of the 2 Samuel 7 passage. Matthew's reference to the kingdom provides further evidence of the connection between these two portions of Scripture: "I will establish his kingdom" (2 Sam. 7:12) and "I will give unto thee the keys of the kingdom" (Matt. 16:19). Although both Mark and Luke record Peter's confession of Jesus as Messiah, only Matthew includes Jesus' extended reply with his reference to the kingdom. Matthew's focus is on the in-breaking of the expected kingdom; the establishment of that kingdom is irrevocably connected to the building of a house – the church.

The third verse of this section is a quotation from Amos 9:11, "I will raise up the tabernacle of David." In Psalm 118:22, David had written, "The stone that the builders disallowed, the same is made the head of the corner." Christ's post-resurrection position at God's right hand is the headstone of which David wrote. Isaiah also refers to this cornerstone, "Behold, I lay in Zion for a foundation a stone, a tried stone, a precious cornerstone, a sure foundation...." (Isa. 28:16). New Testament authors draw upon this imagery, recognizing Jesus as the cornerstone upon which David's tabernacle rests. Upon this foundation stone (1 Cor. 3:11), the builder (Acts 2:47) added living stones to form a spiritual house (1 Pet. 2:5). Paul writes of redeemed Jews and Gentiles as fellow citizens and as the household of God, "built upon the foundation…Jesus Christ himself being the chief cornerstone, in whom all the building fitly framed together groweth unto an holy temple in the Lord; in whom ye also are builded together for an habitation of God through the Spirit" (Eph. 2:20-22). In Revelation 3:7, John records Jesus' words that the key of David is indeed on his shoulder, a reference to Isaiah 22:22. He who possesses this key controls the entrance of subjects into his kingdom, although he authorizes his disciples to act on his behalf (cf. John 20:23; Matt. 16:19, and Acts 26:16-18). The tabernacle of David, prophesied by Amos, finds its fulfillment in the New Testament church, built upon the cornerstone of Jesus Christ.

God is quite clear about **when** he will establish David's throne and kingdom. It is **while David sleeps with the fathers,** or pre-resurrection, that Christ will sit on the throne of David, establish the kingdom, and build God's house (2 Sam. 7:12, 13 and 1 Chron. 17:11, 12). Peter specifically reminded his hearers of this fact on the day of Pentecost when he said, "Men and brethren, let me freely speak unto you of the patriarch, David, that he is both dead and buried, and his sepulcher is with us unto this day" (Acts 2:29). The building of God's house will take place **before** David is raised from the dead. Instead of sitting on David's throne after the resurrection (when David will be awake), Jesus occupies the throne and builds the house while David sleeps.

The book of Hebrews considers the present order to be the final and true fulfillment of God's sovereign purpose; therefore, we must reject an expectation of another age and another temple unless we can find clear evidence in the New Testament Scriptures. Jesus is presently the minister "of the true tabernacle" (Heb. 8:2). The tabernacle of David is established with the "throne of David" (Acts 2:30, 31), "the key of David" (Rev. 3:7), and the "sure mercies of David" (Acts 13:32-34).

Another Priest

"Thou art a priest forever after the order of Melchizedek." (Ps. 110:4b)

"...he shall be a priest upon his throne." (Zech. 6:13)

"...after the similitude of Melchizedek there ariseth another priest." (Heb. 7:15b)

Here again, the Dispensationalist is in a quandary. In order to be consistent with his hermeneutical presuppositions (literal [natural] whenever possible), he faces the problem of the Aaronic priesthood functioning simultaneously with the Melchizedekian priesthood in a millennial age. According to a literal interpretation of Ezekiel 43:19, the predicted kingdom features a renewal of the Aaronic priesthood: "And thou shalt give to the priests, the Levites, who are of the seed of Zadok, who approach unto me, to minister unto me, saith the Lord GOD, a young bullock for a sin offering." The same hermeneutic, applied to Psalm 110, results in a priest after the order of Melchizedek: "The LORD has sworn, and will not repent, Thou art a priest forever after the order of Melchizedek." If the Dispensationalist attributes full Melchizedekian status to Christ now, in the church age, he must forfeit a revival of a functioning Aaronic priesthood when this office is supposed to operate, namely, in the future millennium. Dispensationalism teaches that Christ will be a Melchizedekian priest "in the millennium...to refresh and bless his people."[9]

The book of Hebrews holds the key to understanding the role of the priesthood in any age. The author of Hebrews does not present the possibility of two simultaneous priesthoods, each of a different order. The installment of the Melchizedekian priesthood eliminates the Aaronic priesthood. "For the priesthood being changed, there is made of necessity a change of the law." The reinstitution of the Aaronic priesthood, as well as a return to Old Covenant sacrificial offerings, is a scriptural impossibility. Just as the new and better covenant forever banished the old and weaker covenant, so the new priesthood eclipses the old. The Aaronic priesthood functioned appropriately in its season, under the Old Covenant, but now that a better priesthood, better suited to function under a better covenant has appeared, the old is obsolete. The Old Covenant and the old priesthood are inextricably bound together; therefore, the dissolution of one demands the dissolution of the other. This same principle applies to the New Covenant and the new priesthood: the operation of the first triggers the operation of the second. Knowing these implications, a Dispensationalist takes a deductive approach to the book of Hebrews, which undermines the force of the permanent switch of priesthoods and again subordinates the Scriptures to a preconceived system of theology.

---

9 *Concise Bible Dictionary* (Bible Truth Publishers, 1976) p. 520

God certified the Aaronic priesthood by causing the rod of Levi to bud after it lay overnight in the tabernacle, and thus set aside the possibility of any other tribe occupying the priesthood (Num. 17). So, too, when God raised the "rod of Jesse" after it lay in the tomb for three days, he forever eliminated Levi from claims to the priesthood. Dispensationalists paint a millennial Aaronic priesthood scenario, based on Ezekiel 40-47, and portray the coexistence of this Aaronic priesthood with the Melchizedekian one. The author of Hebrews knows of no such conflation of priesthoods; he sees a distinct change. The idea of a millennial Aaronic priesthood ignores this change and denies the greater revelation of the New Testament. "If he were on earth, he should not be a priest, seeing that there are priests that offer gifts according to the law" (Heb. 8:4). To make the Melchizedekian office function alongside the Aaronic at Jesus' return is to put new wine in old wineskins; it simply cannot be done. The new wine will burst the old skins.

One of the benefits of the New Covenant, which some Dispensationalists believe belongs specifically to Israel alone in the millennial age, is that the people under the covenant "shall teach no more every man his neighbor" because God will have written his law on their hearts (Jer. 31:34). Yet the kingdom described in Ezekiel 44:23, which is millennial in Dispensationalism,[10] includes this charge to

---

[10] "...the preferable interpretation [of Ezekiel 40-48] is that Ezekiel gives a picture of the millennial temple. This interpretation is in keeping with God's prophetic program for the millennium. The

the priests: "Teach my people the difference between the unclean and the clean." To meet consistent Dispensational hermeneutics, the fulfillment of Ezekiel's prophecy must include a return to a restricted priesthood and lists of unclean and clean items and practices. If Ezekiel writes of the kingdom in the millennium, why does he have the priests teaching what the people already know? God has already written his law on his people's hearts; the people have no need for the priests to instruct them. The handy catch basin of all unfulfilled prophecy (i.e., the millennium) does not conform to Dispensational hermeneutics; here, it contradicts them.

The New Testament age emphasizes the saved as a priesthood of believers (1 Pet. 2:5, 9; Rev. 1:6) who are "taught of God" (John 6:45; 1 John 2:27), "know all things" (1 Cor. 1:5; 2:10-16), and "fulfill the law of God" (Rom. 8:4; 13:10; John 14:15; 2 Cor. 3:3, cf. Ezek. 36:26, 27, esp. 27). Will the New Covenant era include instruction by the Levitical priests? According to 1 John 2:27, "the anointing which ye have received of Him abideth in you, and ye need not that any man teach you." Whether one believes that the New Covenant is fulfilled now in the church or awaits a more full and formal fulfillment in a Jewish millennium, one must acknowledge the New Testament teaching on the priesthood. The New Testament Scriptures preclude an interpretation of Ezekiel 44:23 that posits a future priestly class of men, distinct from the rest of the believing popula-

---

Church is not in view here, but rather it is a prophecy for the consummation of Israel's history on earth." *New Scofield*, 884.

tion, who will be the teachers of God's people under the New Covenant. The priesthood of which the Old Testament prophesied operates now, in the New Testament age. All believers are priests, and Jesus Christ is the great High Priest who is "forever after the order of Melchizedek" (Heb. 7:21). A teaching body of priests is discordant with the proleptic promises of Jeremiah 31.

Another King

"A king shall reign in righteousness." (Isa. 32:1)

"And David, my servant, shall be king over them.... My servant, David, shall be their prince forever." (Ezek. 37:24, 25)

"...He...shall rise to reign over the Gentiles." (Isa.11:10, LXX)

Christ functions equally and simultaneously as both king and priest. Christ presently fills the Melchizedekian office of priest; he fills the office of king as well, just as Melchizedek did. Melchizedek was not merely a priest of the Most High God, but also a "king of righteousness and peace" (Heb. 7:1, 2; 2 Chron. 26:16-18). Dispensationalists have difficulty with this kingly aspect of the double office because that relationship to the church seems foreign for them. This present kingship of Christ is another area where Dispensationalists minimize the force of the New Testament's interpretation of the Old Testament.

The historic Dispensationalist would say that the kingship of Christ has no relevance for the church. They insist that Christ is *lord* of the church and *king* of Israel. That kingship has no present realization; it is in hibernation. Christ is exalted as king now, but he does not exercise his reign now. He reserves his kingship for a future coming reign. Christ's kingship is for future restored Israel, who forfeited the kingdom during Christ's first advent, and who thereby compelled Christ to postpone his rule until after the church is raptured. Then, but not before, will his reign begin. "Prophetically, [Psalm 110] looks forward to the time when Christ will appear as the Rod of the LORD's strength, the Deliverer out of Zion (Rom. 11:25-27), and to the conversion of Israel...and to the judgment upon the Gentile powers which precedes the setting up of the kingdom...." [11] "Upon his return the King will restore the Davidic monarchy in His own Person, regather dispersed Israel, establish his power over all the earth, and reign 1000 years." [12]

Citizens of a country are subjects of that country's ruler. The New Testament views Christians as citizens of the kingdom of Christ, transferred there from the kingdom of darkness (Col. 1:13; Eph. 5:5; Matt. 13:24-31; 21:43). When the early apostles and evangelists preached the gospel, they did so in terms of the kingdom of God (Acts 1:3; 8:12; 19:8; 20:24-25; 28:30-31), implying that people in this kingdom belong to the king of it. Paul's preaching that Jesus was king earned him criticism from his listeners in Thessalonica (Acts 17:7). Peter uses kingly language to explain Jesus to the Sanhedrin council in Jerusalem: "Him hath God exalted ...to be a Prince..." (Acts 5:31). The term *prince* (Greek *archēgós*) indicates a leader with inherent authority or the chief leader. Peter interprets Christ's rule as a present occupancy of David's throne; right now, Jesus is on the throne of David (Acts 2:30, 31). Dispensationalists fail to acknowledge that *my [God's] throne* equals *David's throne*

---

[11] Ibid., 655.

[12] Ibid., 1248.

(Rev. 3:21). Their separation of these two thrones is not biblically supportable: the Davidic king sat "on the throne of
the kingdom of the LORD over Israel" (1 Chron. 28:5, cf.
Zech. 6:13, Rev. 3:21; for further evidence, see 1 Chron.
29:23; 2 Chron. 9:8, cf. 1 Kings 2:12; 1 Chron. 17:11-12, cf.
Luke 1:32, 33). The New Testament testifies that Christ now
performs Davidic activities: James sees Jesus as building
"the tabernacle of David" (Acts 15:16, 17), prophesied by
Amos (9:11-12), and Paul sees Jesus as providing "the sure
mercies of David" (Acts 13:32-34), prophesied by Isaiah
(55:3). Why then would we deny Christ the present throne
activity of David?

Some deny this kingship of Jesus because they doubt his
present reign. Is Christ reigning now? Jesus himself describes his activity between advents in terms of reign.
When he, the nobleman, returns, he sentences his enemies
to death because they *had previously rejected his rule over
them.* "Those mine enemies, who would not that I should
reign over them, bring hither; and slay them before me"
(Luke 19:27, emphasis added). Phillips translates: "these
enemies of Mine who objected to My being King over them
…" Jesus frames the parable in terms of kingdom and citi-
zenship: "But his citizens hated him, and sent a message
after him, saying, 'We will not have this man to reign over
us'" (Luke 19:14). Even his enemies recognized his claim to
kingship; they reject him in terms of reign. This reign began
upon his ascension to the throne, "sit thou at my right
hand" (Ps. 110:1), from whence he extends the rod of his
strength "in the midst of [his] enemies" (Ps. 110:2, cf. Matt.

13:24-30). Daniel, in his vision, describes Christ's sessional sitting at his Father's right hand when "...the Son of man came with the clouds of heaven, and came to the Ancient of days, and they brought him near before him. And there was given him...a kingdom...." (Dan. 7:13, 14).

The apostle Paul sees the mediatory reign of Christ as present and efficacious for the church. In Romans 15, he urges Jewish and Gentile unity in the church, explaining that Jesus Christ was a minister to the Jews for two purposes: to confirm the promises made to the patriarchs, and to cause the Gentiles to glorify God for his mercy (15:1-9). Paul then quotes a string of promises from the Old Testament Scriptures, all predicting Gentile praise for the God of Israel. He ends with a quote from Isaiah, couched not in the expected terms of Gentile praise for the offspring of Jesse, but in unexpected terms of the Branch's rule over the Gentiles. "The root of Jesse will come, even he who arises to rule the Gentiles; in him will the Gentiles hope" (Rom. 15:12, cf. Isa. 11:1, 10, ESV). In Paul's mind, the time of his ministry, the time of Gentile praise, and the time of Christ's rule over the Gentiles are concurrent.

The temporarily less-ostentatious reign to which Paul refers in 1 Corinthians 15:25, "He must reign, till he hath put all enemies under his feet," culminates when Christ descends and puts down the last enemy, death (1 Cor. 15: 26, 54). At this point, "the kingdoms of this world are become the kingdoms of our Lord, and of his Christ; and he shall reign for ever and ever" (Rev. 11:15; 22:5). Death will have been swallowed up in victory and all offensive elements will have been forever banished (Rev. 22:15). God will be all in all (1 Cor. 15:28). For Dispensationalists, that future visible reign (1 Tim. 6:14-15) overshadows the present transient stage, perceptible only to the eye of faith: "we see not yet all things put under him (the future reign), but we see Jesus... *crowned* with glory and honor" (the present reign) (Heb. 2:8, 9; Rev. 20:4). "Behold your King," has now become the gaze of all Gentile magi, who come from the east and the west to worship him who was born king, died king, ascended king, and will return king (Matt. 2:2; Mark 15:26; Acts 17:7; Rev. 19:16).

Another Prophet

"The LORD thy God will raise up unto thee a Prophet from the midst of thee, of thy brethren, like unto me, unto him ye shall hearken." (Deut. 18:15)

The Jew's inquiry of John, "Art thou that prophet?" (John 1:21), shows their consciousness of a coming prophet. Many of them, upon hearing Jesus' teaching, confessed, "Of a truth this is the Prophet" (John 7:40). Has that prophet now ceased to speak? Has he cancelled his office because Israel did not know the voices of the prophets? Has the introduction of the church tabled Christ's prophetic office until the next Jewish dispensation arrives? In the same manner that Dispensationalists push Christ's office of king to a future glory day for Israel, they also forestall Christ's office of prophet. Both are inoperative during the present church age. Does this office, like that of priest and king, temporarily cease because national Israel did not recognize it? What do the New Testament Scriptures answer?

God, in times past, had spoken unto the fathers by the prophets (Heb. 1:1), the archetype being Moses himself (John 9:29). Moses' stature was so great that anyone who despised his words died without mercy (Heb. 10:28). Disobedience to Moses resulted in serious consequences: God cut off the rebellious from the faithful (Num. 11; 16; Deut. 1:42-44). God used signs (miracles in Egypt and the glory cloud in the wilderness) to show the people that Moses was his deputed oracle: "They were baptized unto Moses in the cloud" (1 Cor. 10:2).

When the superior prophet came, God used a greater witness to demonstrate to the people that Jesus was the anointed prophet who calls his people into the fold and leads them to an incorruptible inheritance (John 10; 1 Pet. 1:4; Heb. 4:3, cf. Matt. 11:28). God gave his Son the Spirit without measure (John 3:34), by whom the Son cast out demons (Matt. 12:28) and performed many other signs and wonders (John 5:36; Acts 2:22), indicating that "he was worthy of more glory than Moses" (Heb. 3:3). In spite of full evidence, Israel, like Pharaoh, hardened their hearts: yet there remained one last sign for an evil and adulterous generation – "the promise of My Father" (Luke 24:49, cf. Acts 2:33). The ascended Son sends the promised Spirit, through whom the Son speaks (John 14:16-18; 15:26) and by whom the Son proves that he yet lives (Heb. 11:4).

If the consequences of ignoring Moses were severe, how much more severe will be the consequences of ignoring God's own Son? How will anyone escape if he "turn[s] away from him that speaketh from heaven" (Heb. 2:3; 12:25)? The second-covenant prophet, Jesus, eclipses the first-covenant prophet, Moses, by sprinkling his people (1 Pet. 1:2), not with "the blood of calves and of goats" (Heb. 9:19), ratifying a temporary covenant, but with his own precious blood (1 Pet. 1:19), establishing an everlasting covenant (Heb. 13:20).

Having raised Christ (not in incarnation, but in resurrection), God sent him first to Israel to bless them (Acts 3:26), forgive them (Acts 5:31, 32), and give them light (Acts 26:23). In unbroken continuity of that office, Christ is "a light to lighten the Gentiles" (Luke 2:32, cf. Rom. 15:9). That prophetic voice first sounded forth from his own lips in the days of his flesh (Heb. 1:1), then advanced through them that had heard him (Heb. 2:3, 4; 3:15), and now continues through his people (Luke 10:16; John 17:18-20). Christ's prophetic voice echoes *now*, through the whole of the last age, the church age, and is not relegated to some imaginative future age (Eph. 2:14-17; Gal. 4:14; Heb. 1:1, cf. Heb. 9:26; 1 John 2:18; Acts 2:16-21). Therefore, "every soul [Jews], who will not hear that prophet, shall be destroyed from among the *people*" (Acts 3:23, emphasis added).

The *people* are now the elect non-castaways of Israel (Rom. 11:5), the remnant, who remained in the olive tree and became the new nucleus of the New Covenant. Believing Israelites are the ones with whom the Gentiles become fellow heirs. When Gentiles hear the voice of the Prophet, they join the New Covenant community of believers. "Thou, being a wild olive tree, were grafted in *among them*, and *with them* partakest of the root and fatness of the olive tree...." (Rom. 11:17, emphasis added). Here again, Dispensationalists have missed the historical unfolding phenomena of what the Old Testament said would come, by not believing that the prophet like Moses has come and exercises his prophetic office in the church age.

Another Covenant

"This is the covenant that I will make with them after those days." (Jer. 31:33)

It goes unquestioned by any that Jesus inaugurated the New Covenant[13] when he instituted the Lord's Supper, saying, "This is the blood of the new covenant which is shed for many for the remission of sins" (Matt. 26:28). Yet Dispensationalists believe that Christ did not explicitly invest this New Covenant in the church. They overthrow such verses as, "Who also hath made us [Paul and co-workers] able ministers of the new covenant..." (2 Cor. 3:6, cf. Gal. 4:24-26; Heb. 8:6, 13; 9:15) by their understanding of other passages: "Israel, to whom pertaineth...the covenants... and the promises..." (Rom. 9:4; also Heb. 8:8; Eph. 2:12). Dispensationalists claim that these verses restrict the ministries to the Jews, who are the only objects prophecy addresses, and therefore, the ministries of the New Covenant are not intended for the New Testament church. As we consider these verses, we must ask about the identity of the Jews addressed in them. The Dispensationalist quotes the three categories of people Paul mentions in 1 Corinthians 10:32 (the Jews, the Greeks, the church of God)[14] or Gala-

---

[13] Preterism insists that the New Covenant was in force until AD 70.

[14] Paul is not dividing all humanity into three groups. In this passage, he is talking about Christian liberty. A Christian had to be con-

tians 3:28, and reasons that the church is in no way Jewish. Membership in the body of Christ removes the pre-converted nationalities of believers; those Jews outside the church are the true Jews to whom the New Covenant of the future belongs.

How do the Scriptures handle this quandary? The Old Testament foresaw an age when God would install a new and better covenant (Jer. 31:33-34), through which he would instill his Spirit and create new hearts in his people (Ezek. 36:26, 27). Scripture portrays the Jews (nationally) as children of the covenant, whereas the Gentiles are afar off, strangers, foreigners, aliens to the commonwealth of Israel and without hope (Acts 3:25; Rom. 9:4; Eph. 2:12). How then can anyone consider Gentiles as Jews? The answer lies in terms of mystery: not in our English sense of the word as something unfathomable or difficult to unravel, but in the Pauline sense of the word as revelation of that which would otherwise be uncertain.

Paul, who was a prisoner for the Gentiles (Col. 4:3), was in chains because he was carrying the hope of Israel to the Gentiles (Eph. 3:1, cf. Acts 22:21; 28:20). This is the mystery: the nations who once were without hope now have the hope of Israel. God had given external markers of special

---

cerned with not offending the conscience of Jews, of unbelievers (Greeks), and of fellow-Christians. If Paul were writing today to saints working in Saudi Arabia, or to Christian soldiers in Iraq, he would not mention Jews, but he would say, "Be careful not to offend the Muslims, the Greeks (unbelievers), or your fellow-believers."

nation status solely to Israel; if he had not revealed that the Gentiles were to partake of the same hope as Israel, who would have known? There was no evidence apart from revelation. Believing Gentiles are "fellow heirs and of the same body" (with believing Israel – NIV, Eph. 3:6), "partakers of their spiritual things" (Rom. 15:27), "with *them* partakest of the root and fatness of the olive tree" (Rom. 11:17), and "fellow citizens of the saints [Jewish saints]" (Eph. 2:19).

The Old Testament Scriptures indicated that in a coming day, God would include Gentiles with his people (Isa. 19:16-24). The mystery is not that God will bless Gentiles along with Israel, but that neither the Gentiles nor Israel will come into covenant relationship with God via Judaism. In the New Covenant, the only route to a covenant relationship with God is through Christ (Isa. 42:6; 49:6; Acts 13:46; Heb. 12:24; Gal. 6:15-16). The Old Testament Scriptures hint at this; the New Testament Scriptures explain it more clearly. Paul tells us, "not all Israel is of Israel" (Rom. 9:6), indicating that true Israel alone is the beneficiary of the covenants and the promises. The Jews who "stumbled at the stumbling stone" and did not profit by the preached Word (Heb. 4:2) were spiritually uncircumcised and lost their rights to the New Covenant and Abrahamic promise. "They who are the children of the flesh [ethnic Jews], these are not the children of God, but the children of promise are counted as the seed" (Rom. 9:8). Scripture defines "children of the promise" not as those "born after the flesh" (Gal. 4:29), but as all believers, Gentile as well as Jewish, who,

like Isaac, are "born after the Spirit" (Gal. 4:29). "The promise is unto you [Jews]…and to all that are afar off [Gen-
tiles]" (Acts 2:39; John 10:16; Gal. 3:14). One aspect of the
mystery about which Paul writes is that the church (con-
sisting of believing Gentiles and Jews) is the precise recipi-
ent of the second covenant.

Paul describes believers in the church age as "Jews in-
wardly" (Rom. 2:28-29) who are "circumcised with the circumcision made without hands" (Col. 2:11). The New Testament covenant community "is the real circumcision, who
worship by the Spirit of God" (Phil. 3:3, ESV). Believers are
"Abraham's seed and heirs according to the promise" (Gal.
3:27-29), "who the *scriptures* saw *afore* to be blessed" (Gal.
3:8, cf. Mark 16:15). Believing Jews and Gentiles together
constitute "a royal priesthood and holy nation" (1 Pet. 2:9),
who "come to Mt. Zion…and to the mediator of the new
covenant" (Heb. 12:22-24), belong to "the Jerusalem above"
(Gal. 4:26), and are "a nation bringing forth the fruits of
[the kingdom]" (Matt. 21:43): the *TRUE* "Israel of God"
(Gal. 6:16; Rev. 12:6-17).

The ministry of the apostle Paul, a minister of the New
Covenant (2 Cor. 3:6), verifies that the New Covenant is for
the church and is not for national Israel. At the very outset
of his ministry, he is commissioned by the Lord Jesus, "…I
have appeared unto thee for this purpose, to make thee a
minister…[for] the people [Jews], and Gentiles, unto whom
now I send thee, to open their eyes, and to turn them from
darkness to light, and from the power of Satan unto
God…." (Acts 26:16-18). Carefully compare these words

about Paul's ministry with the Old Testament language of the then-future New Covenant. "I...will give thee for a covenant of the people [Israel], for a light of the Gentiles; to open the blind eyes, to bring out the prisoners from the prison, and those who sit in darkness out of the prison house" (Isa. 42:6, 7, cf. Luke 4:18). Although the similarity of language is obvious, Isaiah refers only to Jesus' ministry. How does Isaiah's prophecy about a light to the Gentiles fit Jesus, since Jesus limited his ministry primarily to the lost sheep of Israel (Matt. 10:5, 6; Rom. 15:8)?

Jesus, in his first advent, did not aim his light at the Gentiles (Matt. 15:22-27). Did Jesus' testifying end at Calvary? Just as a double portion of Elijah's spirit fell upon Elisha, the Spirit of the Lord God anointed Jesus and then fell upon the church (Acts 2). Jesus' ministry was "to proclaim liberty to the captives and the opening of the prison to them that are bound [Israel]" (Isa. 61:1). Jesus appointed and anointed his followers to do "greater works" (John 14:12), to extend that proclamation to all who are captive, i.e., to make disciples of all nations (Matt. 28:19). The mantle of Christ fell upon his apostles; they were to gather the other sheep (Gentiles), which "I [Jesus] must bring" (John 10:16).

Jesus Christ began to preach the gospel of great salvation in person; he continued to preach, post-ascension, through his disciples, who "went everywhere preaching the word" (Acts 8:4, cf. Heb. 2:3, 4). Jesus not only commissioned them; he also accompanied them: "and lo I am with you always" (Matt. 28:20). The Lord "work[ed] with them"

(Mark 16:20), so that whoever heard them, heard him (Luke 10:16). His accompaniment was more than simply assistance; it was appearance – via his ambassadors (2 Cor. 5:20; Eph. 6:20; Gal. 4:14). Paul wrote to the Ephesians, "He [Christ Jesus] is our peace...who came and preached peace to you [the Ephesian Gentiles] which were afar off...." (Eph. 2:14, 17). Jesus went to Ephesus, not in his incarnate body, but by way of his Spirit, through his spirit-filled oracles (1 Pet. 1:10-12).

Jesus fulfilled Isaiah's prophecy as both the glory of his people Israel and as "a light to lighten the Gentiles" (Luke 2:32). Paul presents Jesus Christ as "a minister of the circumcision for the truth of God, to confirm the promises made unto the fathers [this he did in the days of his flesh, cf. Matt. 5:17] and that the Gentiles might glorify God for his mercy; as it is written, For this cause I will confess to thee among the Gentiles.... He that shall rise to reign over the Gentiles; in him shall the Gentiles trust" (Rom. 15:8-12). Paul, citing Isaiah, attributes both ministries to the Lord Jesus; Christ executes the later ministry to the Gentiles through his Spirited-guided missionaries (Acts 8:26; 11:12; 18:9-11). Christ ministers to Gentile God-fearers (Acts 10:35; 13:26) so that they "might rejoice with his people" (Rom. 15:10), Israelites who believed ("the Jew first"), and "gain an inheritance among them which are sanctified" by faith in Jesus (Acts 20:32; 26:18).

Paul, Jesus' chosen vessel particularly for the Gentiles, describes this post-resurrection ministry of Christ in terms of Christ's giving direct revelation and making divine appointment (Acts 22:18; 1 Cor. 11:23; 1 Tim. 2:7). Paul viewed his own ministry to the Gentiles as an extension and completion of Christ's ministry to them. "[I] now rejoice in my sufferings for you, and fill up that which is behind of the afflictions of Christ...to fulfill the Word of God" (Col. 1:24-25). The fulfilling of the Word of God was that Gentiles were included in the glad tidings that God had designed for all nations (Luke 2:10; Acts 1:8). Isaiah writes of beautiful feet that bear good tidings (Isa. 52:7): Jesus' feet brought good tidings to the circumcised; his disciples' feet extended those good tidings to the uncircumcised. Jesus had enlisted his followers as preachers for that very end (Rom. 10:14-17).

Luke, in the book of Acts, recounts the pattern described by Paul, "Christ...should rise from the dead, to show light unto the people [Acts 1-7 – Jerusalem, Judea], and to the Gentiles [Acts 8ff. – Samaria and the uttermost parts of the earth]" (Acts 26:23). The Lord Jesus so involves Paul and Barnabas in his own ministry that they rightly consider their missionary travels as his: "...the Lord commanded *us*, saying, I have set thee to be a light of the Gentiles, that thou shouldest be for salvation unto the ends of the earth" (Acts 13:47, cf. Isa. 49:6). It is in this manner that Jesus mediates the New Covenant (Heb. 12:24), which is for all humankind (Jew and Gentile) who believe (1 Tim. 2:4, 5).

The Scriptures do not contemplate the church as an inter-covenantal people or a non-covenantal people. Dispensationalists insist that the risen Lord gave Paul revelation of truths hidden *from* the Old Testament Scriptures, making the church an entirely segregated company from Old Testament hopes. The New Testament Scriptures testify that the ascended Christ gave Paul revelation of truths hidden *in* the Hebrew Scriptures. During his interrogation before Felix, Paul explains the Old Testament origin of his ideas, "...after the way which they call heresy, so worship I the God of my fathers, believing all things which are **written in the law and in the prophets**" (Acts 24:14, emphasis added).

The Jewish leaders arrested Paul because his preaching to the Gentiles (cf. Acts 22:21, 22) was breaking down the middle wall between believing Jews and Gentiles and making them together one new man (Eph. 3:1ff.). The content of his preaching was not extraneous to the Old Testament Scriptures, as Dispensationalists would have us believe. Paul grounds his defense before Agrippa in the Hebrew Scriptures, our Old Testament, "I continue...witnessing... saying *no other* things than *those* which the prophets and Moses did say **should** come...." (Acts 26:22, emphasis added, cf. 1 Cor. 15:3). In Paul's statement, we find the two claims that form the thesis of this paper: (1) Paul derived the subject matter of his preaching strictly from the Old Testament Scriptures and not from that which was foreign to them or innovative on Paul's part. (2) The Old Testament anticipated an age that should come, which Paul says had arrived in his day. If the age to come arrived in Paul's day, then it is not postponed until after the church's removal.

Further verification of these two points comes from Acts 13:26-34, where Paul addresses Jews and Gentiles saying, "the promise which was made unto the fathers God hath fulfilled the same unto *us* [Gentiles included, cf. v. 26; 1 Cor. 10:1]...saying I will give you the sure mercies of David" (vv. 32, 34). Jesus Christ makes good the 'Jewish' promises to Gentile God-fearers, beginning in Paul's day and extending to the present time. The church age is the designated time of fulfilling Old Testament prophecies – we presently have the "sure mercies of David." Right now, Gentile believers are "rejoicing with his people" (Rom. 15:10, cf. Deut. 32:43). James, in the Jerusalem council, as well as Paul, in Pisidian Antioch, recognizes the gospel successes as answering to the prophetic building of the "tabernacle of David" (Acts 15:16, 17).

Dispensationalists face yet another substantial difficulty. They have to reconcile the reinstitution of sin offerings in Ezekiel's temple with God's statement to his second-covenant people that he will remember their sins no more (Jer. 31:34b, cf. Ezek. 43:19, 21, 22, 25). Dispensationalist doctrine clashes with the truth of the New Testament Scriptures, "There remaineth no more sacrifice for sins" (Heb. 10:26b); also, "There is no more offering for sins" (Heb. 10:18b). To have future sin offerings is to make the Scripture deny itself and to send the people of God back into the camp from whence he called them (Heb. 13:13).

This present age is the day of salvation (2 Cor. 6:2, cf. Isa. 49:8) that the prophets prophesied (Rom. 1:1, 2) and the gospel now reveals (1 Pet. 1:10-12; Rom. 16:25, 26). The age to which the Old Testament prophets pointed is realized now; therefore, "Beware lest that come upon you [*you* are the New Testament-age people (Jew and Gentile) to whom Paul is preaching] which is spoken of in the prophets...I work a work *in your days*" (Acts 13:40, 41, emphasis added). Since the prophesied age of salvation is the current age, where is the justification for a subsequent Jewish age? The final age converged on the Pentecost believers, "the church upon whom the end of the ages is come" (1 Cor. 10:11, RSV). The church therefore must be the object of the Old Testament prophecy about the New Covenant that God promised he would make in a coming day.

Another Shaking

"Yet once...and I will shake the heavens, and the earth...." (Hag.2:6, quoted in Heb. 12:26)

Premillenialists as well as amillenialists acknowledge that the age when the overt kingdom of Christ displaces the present covert age (Luke 17:20) is yet future. As Christians, we now enjoy a dimension of "righteousness, peace and joy in the Holy Ghost" (Rom. 14:17) in the present stage of the kingdom; yet we anticipate the prospect of a fuller display in the future stage of the kingdom. We "taste of the heavenly gift...and of the powers [which are but foreshadows] of the age to come" now (Heb. 6:4, 5, cf. Matt. 12:32; Eph. 1:14). Paul encouraged the disciples, "we must through much tribulation enter into the kingdom of God" (Acts 14:22, also 2 Thess. 1:5), and Peter desired his readers to have an abundant entrance into the future everlasting kingdom (2 Pet. 1:11).

The Old Testament prophets spoke of not only the age's duration while "the heavens must receive him" (the church age, Acts 3:21), but also the age's extension after the Lord returns to "reign for ever and ever" (Rev. 11:15-18; 22:5; Isa. 65:17ff., cf. 2 Pet. 3:10-13). Dispensationalists have failed to recognize that the present age consumes all the *economic* passages of prophecy (such as we have dealt with in this book), whereas the age to come will consume all the *theonomic* passages (such as Job 19:25-27; Psa. 17:15; Isa. 65:17;

Rev. 1:7; Jude 14; and 1 Cor. 15:28 [this is a representative list and is not intended to be exhaustive]).

The entire created order waits for the 'another shaking.' "The whole creation groaneth and travaileth in pain together" (Rom. 8:22); relief from this condition will occur precisely when the sons of God are manifest and receive their new bodies (Rom. 8:23, 1 Cor. 15:51ff). At Jesus' return, death (the last enemy) is destroyed and the whole of creation enters into its glorious liberty. According to Paul, in 1 Corinthians 15:50-55, God's believing people, both dead and alive, need new bodies because flesh and blood cannot inherit the kingdom of God. When do believers receive these new bodies? The trumpet sounds, the believing dead rise with new bodies, and the believing living follow suit. When this event occurs, death is swallowed up in victory; it is destroyed. If the last enemy, death, is destroyed at the time of the resurrection, and if the resurrection is truly, as Jesus said 'the last day,' then no Dispensational doctrine of a post-resurrection interim state or Jewish millennium with its mixture of good and bad, life and death, has any support in the New Testament.

Conclusion

Dispensational literalism does not allow Jesus Christ and his writing disciples to provide a new perspective for interpreting the Old Testament and is therefore oriented to the Old Covenant rather than to the cross. The Old Testament prophecies repeatedly refer to sin offerings, sacrifices, priests, sabbath-keeping, circumcision, and the Passover; these symbolically point to the character of the New Covenant, not to the actual practices of the New Covenant. The cross and resurrection of Christ irrevocably transform the nature of Israel and all her eschatological fulfillments. Christian authors of Scripture frequently transcend the literal, historical meaning of Jewish Scriptures and give them new light. As Vern Poythress points out, "Dispensationalism's weakness is neglecting the integration of typological interpretation with grammatical-historical interpretation."[15]

Since many of today's Dispensationalists generally adopt an 'already-not yet'[16] view of fulfillment, it would not surprise me if this work did not elicit much disagreement from them. They may not see themselves as those at whom the arguments in this book are aimed. Indeed, they may even echo some of the assertions I have made. Alt-

---

[15] Vern F. Poythress, *Understanding Dispensationalists* (Grand Rapids, MI: Zondervan, 1987), 115.

16 Bateman, Three Central Issues, 33.

hough some readers may draw implications to the contrary, the purpose of this work is not to refute a two-stage coming of Christ, a seven-year tribulation, the restoration of Israel and her place in prophecy, the land promises, or a premillennial view. These are doctrines about which all brands of Dispensationalists would be sensitive. My intent is to stress the absolute authority and finality the New Testament must have upon our understanding of the Old Testament.

New Covenant Theology's dispute with Dispensationalism is not with whether Jews will be converted in masses in the days prior to the Parousia; this should seem evident from Romans 11. (Although I may not use the same language as Dispensationalists in describing this regrafting of Israel into the olive tree, I agree in substance with them.) Jewish conversion is not a dividing point between Dispensational, New Covenant, or even Reformed theologians. If I have adequately demonstrated by the New Testament that the New Covenant period has fulfilled certain key prophecies of the Old Testament, then what justification would dissenters have for a post-New Covenant-age fulfillment of those same prophecies? Nor is the controversy over whether there will be a fuller future reign of Christ, in either a one-thousand year terminus or in an endless kingdom; rather, it addresses the best biblical hermeneutic that gives the New Testament its proper hearing and allows the student of Scripture to be consistent with biblical revelation. Whatever the post-advent period looks like, it will be frosting on the cake, rather than returning the cake to the oven and rebaking it. New Covenant Theology, above all other theological systems available to modern scholarship, comes closest to giving Christ his glorious preeminence and his Holy Spirit-inspired New Testament authors their decisive place in biblical interpretation.

Bibliography

Barcellos, Richard. *In Defense Of The Decalogue: A Critique Of New Covenant Theology.* Enumclaw, WA: WinePress Publishing, 2001.

Bateman, Herbert W. IV, ed. *Three Central Issues in Contemporary Dispensationalism.* Grand Rapids, MI: Kregel Publications, 1999.

Concise Bible Dictionary. N.D. Reprint, Oak Park, IL: Bible Truth Publishers, 1976.

Gerstner, John. *Wrongly Dividing the Word of Truth.* Brentwood, TN: Wolgemuth & Hyatt, 1991.

Larkin, Clarence. *Dispensational Truth.* Philadelphia, PA: Rev. Clarence Larkin est., 1918: 151. Quoted in Herbert W. Bateman IV, *Three Central Issues* (Grand Rapids, MI: Kregel Publications, 1999), 31.

Poythress, Vern F. *Understanding Dispensationalists.* Grand Rapids, MI: Zondervan, 1987.

MacArthur, John, ed. *The MacArthur Study Bible.* Nashville, TN: Word Bible, 1997.

Reisinger, John G. "Review of *In Defense of the Decalogue,*" *Sound of Grace* 9:6 (April 2003) – 10:6 (April 2004).

Scofield, C. I., ed. *The New Scofield Reference Bible.* NY: Oxford University Press, 1967.

Wells, Tom, and Fred Zaspel. *New Covenant Theology: Description, Definition, Defense.* Frederick, MD: New Covenant Media, 2002.

www.ingramcontent.com/pod-product-compliance
Lightning Source LLC
Chambersburg PA
CBHW060144050426
42448CB00010B/2297